MW01295522

THE CONSTELLATIONS
Myths of the Stars

Errol Jud Coder

Written by Errol Jud Coder
Cover Design and Illustrations by Errol Jud Coder

© 2012 Errol Jud Coder

No part of this book may be reproduced in any form for any electronic or mechanical means, including information storage and retrieval devices or systems, without prior written permission, except that brief passages may be quoted for reviews.

Printed in the United States
10 9 8 7 6 5 4 3 2 1

March 2012

ISBN-13:
978-1475030785

ISBN-10:
1475030789

:Mythology:
Astronomy, Myths
Adult, Young Adult & Juvenile

NOTE Every effort has been taken to ensure that all information in this book is correct and accurate. Contact us with any mistakes that you might find.

CONTENTS

1

Introduction

Most ancient cultures saw pictures in the stars of the night sky. The earliest known efforts to catalog the stars date to cuneiform texts and artifacts dating back roughly 6000 years. These remnants, found in the valley of the Euphrates River, suggest that the ancients observing the heavens saw the lion, the bull, and the scorpion in the stars. The constellations as we know them today are undoubtedly very different from those first few--our night sky is a compendium of images from a number of different societies, both ancient and modern. By far, though, we owe the greatest debt to the mythology of the ancient Greeks and Romans.

The earliest references to the mythological significance of the Greek constellations may be found in the works of Homer, which probably date to the 7th century B.C. In the Iliad, for instance, Homer describes the creation of Achilleus's shield by the craftsman god Hephaistos:

On it he made the earth, and sky, and sea, the weariless sun and the moon waxing full, and all the constellations that crown the heavens, Pleiades and Hyades, the mighty Orion and the Bear, which men also call by the name of Wain: she wheels round in the same place and watches for Orion, and is the only one not to bathe in Ocean (Iliad XVIII 486-490).

At the time of Homer, however, most of the constellations were not associated with any particular myth, hero, or god. They were instead known simply as the objects or animals which they represented--the Lyre, for instance, or the Ram. By the 5th century B.C., however, most of the constellations had come to be associated with myths, and the Catasterismi of Eratosthenes completed the mythologization of the stars. " At this stage, the fusion between astronomy and mythology is so complete that no further distinction is made between them"

--the stars were no longer merely identified with certain gods or heroes, but actually were perceived as divine (Seznec, 37-40).

Despite the many mentions of the stars in Greek and early Roman texts, by far the most thorough star catalog from ancient times belongs to the Roman Ptolemy of Alexandria, who grouped 1022 stars into 48 constellations during the 2nd century A.D. Although Ptolemy's Almagest does not include the constellations which may only be seen from the southern hemisphere, it forms the basis for the modern list of 88 constellations officially designated by the International Astronomical Union (Pasachoff, 134-135). The influence of both the Greek and Roman cultures may be plainly seen; the myths behind the constellations date back to ancient Greece, but we use their Latin names.

Andromeda

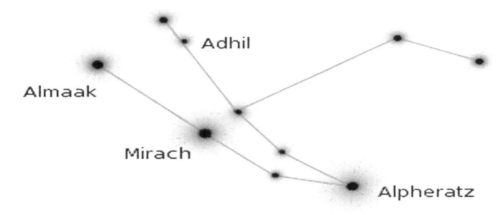

THE PRINCESS

Andromeda was the princess of Ethiopia, daughter of Cepheus and Cassiopeia. Cassiopeia was a boastful woman, and foolishly bragged that she was more beautiful than Hera, the queen of the gods, and the Nereids. In order to avenge the insult to his nymphs, Poseidon sent a sea monster to ravage the Ethiopian coast. (Some accounts state that the constellation Cetus represents the sea monster, but a more common view of Cetus is that he is a peaceful whale.)

The horrified king consulted Ammon, the oracle of Zues, who said that Poseidon could be appeased only by sacrificing Cassiopeia's beautiful virgin daughter, Andromeda, to the monster. Andromeda was duly chained to a rock on the coast, fully exposed to the monster. Fortunately for her, the hero Perseus happened to be flying by on his way back from killing the Gorgon Medusa:

When Perseus saw the princess, her arms chained to the

hard rock, he would have taken her for a marble statue, had not the light breeze stirred her hair, and warm tears streamed from her eyes. Without realizing it, he fell in love. Amazed at the sight of such rare beauty, he stood still in wonder, and almost forgot to keep his wings moving in the air. As he came to a halt, he called out: "You should not be wearing such chains as these--the proper bonds for you are those which bind the hearts of fond lovers! Tell me your name, I pray, and the name of your country, and why you are in chains."

At first she was silent; for, being a girl, she did not dare to speak to a man. She would have concealed her face modestly behind her hands, had they not been bound fast. What she could do, she did, filling her eyes with starting tears. When Perseus persisted, questioning her again and again, she became afraid lest her unwillingness to talk might seem due to guilt; so she told him the name of her country, and her own name, and she also told him how her mother, a beautiful woman, had been too confident in her beauty.

Before she had finished, the waters roared and from the ocean wastes there came a menacing monster, its breast covering the waves far and wide. The girl screamed. Her sorrowing father was close at hand, and her mother too. They were both in deep distress, though the mother had more cause to be so (Metamorphoses IV 674-692).

Perseus tells Andromeda's parents that he'll kill the monster if they agree to give him their daughter's hand in marriage. They of course give him their consent, and Perseus kills the monster. (His exact method of doing so varies in different versions of the myth. Ovid has Perseus stab the monster to death after a drawn-out, bloody battle, while other versions have the hero simply hold up the head of Medusa, turning the monster to stone.) Andromeda is freed, and the two joyously marry.

𝕬𝖓𝖙𝖑𝖎𝖆

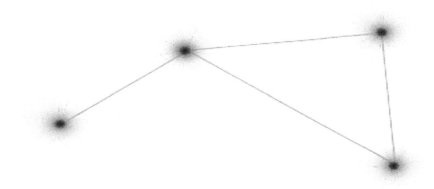

THE WATER PUMP

𝕬ntlia is one of many constellations introduced by Nicolas Louis de Lacaille in the mid eighteenth century, designed to fill in the southern hemisphere. The constellation commemorates the air pump, which had been recently invented by Robert Boyle.

Antlia is located in a rather bleak and lonely part of the southern hemisphere. It takes some imagination to find a "pump" here, not surprising perhaps, given the small selection of Bayer stars.

Apus

BIRD OF PARADISE

Apus is one of those small and inconsequential constellations adapted from others in 1603 by Johann Bayer, designed to fill in the blanks in the Southern Hemisphere. Apart from several binaries and a faint globular cluster little else is found in this portion of the southern skies.

Apus, or Bird of Paradise, was known from sixteenth century voyagers, also being called "Apus Indica" or Bird of India. Some say it comes from the Greek apous, meaning without feet, as a reference to a Greek myth about the swallow, which was said to be legless.

From the paucity of interesting elements in this constellation, it might be argued that the name comes from the Greek apousia, which means "absence".

Aquarius

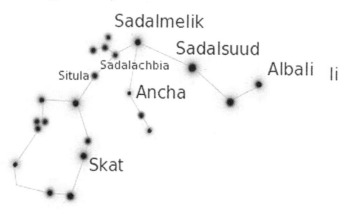

Sadalmelik

Sadalsuud

Sadalachbia

Situla

Albali

li

Ancha

Skat

THE WATER CARRIER

The water carrier represented by the zodiacal constellation Aquarius is Ganymede, a beautiful Phrygian youth. Ganymede was the son of Tros, king of Troy (according to Lucian, he was also son of Dardanus). While tending his father's flocks on Mount Ida, Ganymede was spotted by Zeus. The king of gods became enamored of the boy and flew down to the mountain in the form of a large bird, whisking Ganymede away to the heavens. Ever since, the boy has served as cupbearer to the gods. Ovid has Orpheus sing the tale:

"The king of the gods was once fired with love for Phrygian Ganymede, and when that happened Zeus found another shape preferable to his own. Wishing to turn himself into a bird, he none the less scorned to change into any save that which can carry his thunderbolts. Then without delay, beating the air on borrowed pinions, he snatched away the shepherd of Ilium, who even now mixes the winecups, and supplies Jove with nectar, to the annoyance of Hera".

9

Aquila

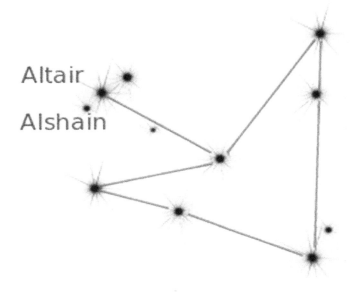

Altair

Alshain

THE EAGLE

Aquila, The Eagle, is another ancient constellation whose history is linked to the Greek gods. The most often-told story is that of Hebe, daughter of Zeus and Hera, who married Heracles.

Before her marriage Hebe was the goddess of youth and she appeared in ceremonies as the official cup bearer. (That's to say, in all religious functions, she was responsible for pouring the wine.) She gave up the post after her marriage (although some accounts say that in one ceremony she indelicately exposed herself and was promptly sacked). In any case, the position was open and Zeus sought a suitable replacement. Ganymede, a splendid Trojan prince, was Zeus's eventual choice.

Zeus either disguised himself as an eagle or sent his Royal Eagle. Ganymede was plucked from his native land and taken to Mount Olympus where he became the wine-pourer for all the gods.

This explains why Ganymede is Zeus's brightest and largest companion: Zeus of course being the Roman name for Zeus.

The constellation Aquila is supposed to represent the eagle carrying away the youth. There are four or five fairly bright stars just below the asterism which are meant to represent the boy (this asterism is called "Antinous" but is not recognised any longer).

Eventually Zeus put Ganymede's own image in the skies, as the god's water bearer, Aquarius.

Ara

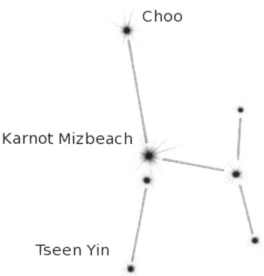

Choo

Karnot Mizbeach

Tseen Yin

THE ALTAR

Ara (The Altar) commemorates the altar on which sacrifices were made to the gods, in both Greek and Roman times. The Romans called it Ara Centauri, considering it to represent the altar Centaurus used (perhaps to sacrifice Lupus, the Wolf).

Aries

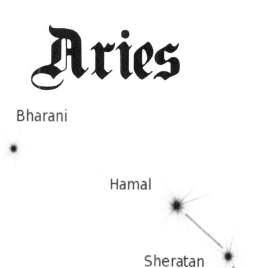

Bharani

Hamal

Sheratan

THE RAM

Aries is a zodiacal constellation representing the ram of the Golden Fleece sought by Jason and the Argonauts. The ram had originally been presented to Nephele by Mercury when her husband took a new wife, Ino, who persecuted Nephele's children. To keep them safe, Nephele sent Phrixus and Helle away on the back of the magical ram, who flew away to the east. Helle fell off into the Hellespont (now the Dardanelles) between the Aegean Sea and the Sea of Marmara, but Phrixus safely made it to Colchis on the eastern shore of the Black Sea. Phrixus sacrificed the ram and presented the Golden Fleece to the king, Aeetes.

Auriga

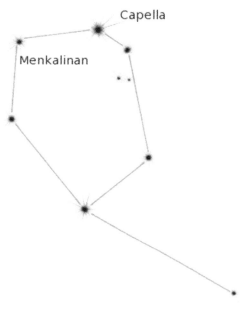

Capella

Menkalinan

THE CHARIOTEER

Auriga is an ancient Northern Hemisphere constellation featuring one of the brightest stars in the heavens: Capella. Auriga is usually pictured as a charioteer; the youth Auriga wields a whip in one hand and holds a goat (Capella) and her two kids in the other.

Bootes

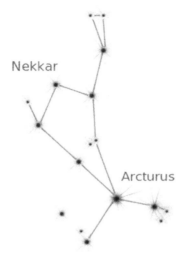

THE HERDSMAN

Boötes may be a hunter, on the tracks of the Great Bear, accompanied by his two dogs Asterion and Chara (the "Canes Venatici"). And yet the constellation was once known as Arctophylax which means the protector of the Bear. Perhaps it was the Romans who changed his role, for they called him Venator Ursae: the Bear Hunter.

Nowadays Boötes is generally considered to be a Herdsman (as in French: Le Bouvier), as he eternally shepherds the stars around the North Pole.

The constellation was known in antiquity, with the first recorded appearance being in Homer's Odyssey. In Book V Odysseus sails his ship by the stars, using the Pleiades, the Bear, and Boötes ("which set late") to reach his destination.

15

Caelum

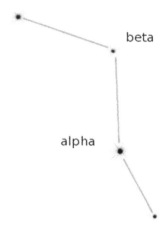

THE HEAVENS

Like many southern hemisphere constellations, Caelum was introduced by Nicolas Louis de Lacaille in the mid-eighteenth century, designed to fill in the southern hemisphere.

The word is ambiguous; in Latin caelum means both "the heavens" and "burin", which is an instrument used for engraving on copper and fine metals. It is this instrument that Lacaille had in mind when he named the constellation.

In fact Lacaille drew two of these instruments in his original map, calling the constellation "Les Burins". Only one has remained.

Camelopardalis

alpha

beta

THE GIRAFFE

If one were asked to name all the four-legged creatures found in the sky, the Ram and the Bull would come readily to mind, and the Bear and Dog (two of each actually: major and minor). A little more thought might produce the Hare (or Rabbit) and the Unicorn (however mythic it might be). Then some might recall that there is also a Fox and a Wolf. And yes, could there also be a Camel?

Not really. The Camel doesn't belong in our menagerie. Camelopardalis means Giraffe. It is also sometimes written Camelopardus, although the correct spelling is indeed CAMELOPARDALIS. At least that's the

17

way Pliny the Elder wrote the animal's name in his Natural History.

The constellation does look like a giraffe, sort of, if you can manage to join together some rather faint stars.

In the winter months the Giraffe appears upside down. You might want to study Camelopardalis in the summer, when it's right side up.

The constellation was probably invented by Petrus Plancius (1552-1622), a Dutchman who made his name in cartography while working for the Dutch East India Company. His world maps of 1592 and 1594 became very popular, while his contribution to the heavenly maps was awarded in 1624 when Camelopardalis was included in Jakob Bartsch's book on the constellations. (Some historians believe Bartsch to have invented the constellation.)

Cancer

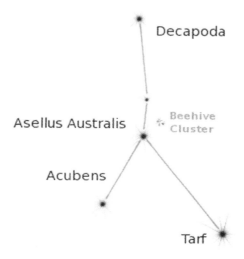

Decapoda

Asellus Australis

Beehive Cluster

Acubens

Tarf

THE CRAB

Cancer is a zodiacal constellation. As with many other constellations, its exact mythological origin is uncertain; however, the most widely accepted story is that Cancer was the crab sent to harass Heracles while he was on his second labor. As he battled the Lernaean Hydra, the ever-jealous Hera sent Cancer to nip at the hero's heels. The crab was eventually crushed beneath Heracles's feet, but Hera placed it in the heavens as a reward for its faithful service.

Cancer may be found between the constellations of Leo and Gemini.

Canes Venatici

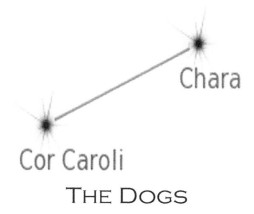

Chara

Cor Caroli

THE DOGS

Canes Venatici is one of those obscure constellations introduced by Johannes Hevelius in 1690. It represents the two dogs Asterion and Chara, both held on a leash by Bootes as they apparently chase the Great Bear around the North Pole.

Canis Major

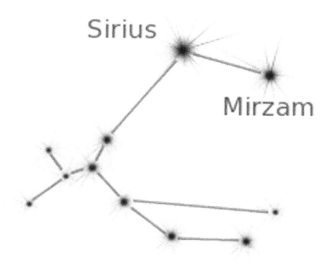

Sirius

Mirzam

THE BIG DOG

Canis Major, the largest of Orion's two hunting dogs, might be chasing Lepus, the Rabbit, who is just in front of him. Or perhaps he is ready to help Orion battle the great bull.

The stories concerning Orion's dogs are not of mythic proportion, but the Greeks did have several interesting beliefs concerning Sirius, alpha Canis Majoris.

The Athenian New Year began with the appearance of Sirius. He was seen as two-headed, like the Roman God Janus: looking back at the past year and forward to the new one.

Sirius was sometimes confused with another two-headed beast called Orthrus. This was Geryon's watchdog;

his job was to guard this tyrant's cattle. Heracles captured the cattle (as his Tenth Labour), killing Orthrus in the process.

In antiquity, as Homer and Hesiod were penning their stories, the Dog Star was already associated with the Sun, since the Sun enters that part of the sky in the hot summer months. While the brightest of stars, it hadn't the best of reputations in antiquity as it was said to bring sickness and death. Perhaps this was due to the fact that July and August were habitually the times of drought and disease.

The name Sirius may come from the Greek meaning "scorching", or it may not. Burnham's Celestial Handbook (as always) offers a wide background into the matter of etymology. The star is mostly thought of now as a winter star, accompanying Orion, rather than as the summer home of the sun.

Canis Minor

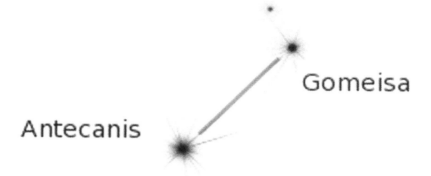

The Little Dog

Canis Minor is sometimes connected with the Teumessian Fox, a beast turned into stone with its hunter, Laelaps, by Zeus, who placed them in heaven as Canis Major (Laelaps) and Canis Minor (Teumessian Fox).

Capricornus

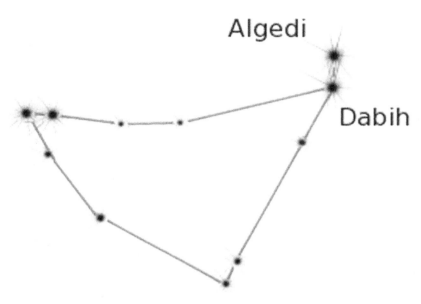

Algedi

Dabih

THE SEA GOAT

This zodiacal constellation, like Pisces, depicts the result of the sudden appearance of the earthborn giant Typhoeus. Bacchus was feasting on the banks of the Nile at the time, and jumped into the river. The part of him that was below water was transformed into a fish, while his upper body became that of a goat. From this point of view, he saw that Typhoeus was attempting to tear Zeus into pieces; he blew a shrill note on his pipes, and Typhoeus fled. Zeus then placed the new shape of Bacchus in the heavens out of thanks for the rescue. Capricornus has therefore from antiquity been represented by a figure with the head and body of a goat and the tail of a fish. It may be seen between Aquarius and Sagittarius low on the southern horizon.

Carina

Canopus

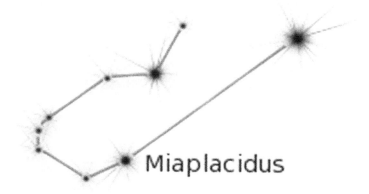

Miaplacidus

THE KEEL

When the twins Castor and Pollux went off with Jason and the rest of the Argonauts, they sailed in the Argo, a ship built by Argus. This ship, equipt with fifty oars and manned by fifty of the best men of Greece, sailed to Colchis, which was at the eastern shore of the Black Sea.

After many adventures Jason (with Medea's help) stole the fleece from the dragon and they all sailed back home.

Athene is said to have commemorated the event by placing their ship, Argo Navis, in the sky as a giant constellation below and east of Canis Major. What is known is that Edmund Halley's catalog of the southern stars, Catalogus stellarum australium (1679), introduced Argo

Navis to the world.

In 1763 Nicolas Louis de Lacaille's posthumous work Caelum australe stelliferum gave us most of the constellations we now know in the southern hemisphere. Lacaille divided the gigantic Argo Navis into three constellations: Carina (the Keel), Puppis (the Stern, or Poop deck), and Vela (the Sail). To this day the Bayer letters (Greek letters) are divided among these three. By far the most interesting of these three is Carina.

Carina is home to Canopus (alpha Carinae), the second brightest star in the heavens.

Cassiopeia

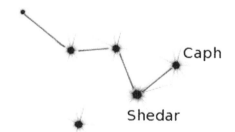

Caph

Shedar

THE QUEEN OF ETHIOPIA

Cassiopeia was the beautiful wife of Cepheus, king of Ethiopia, and the mother of Andromeda. She is most famous in connection with the myth of her daughter, Andromeda. The queen made the mistake of bragging she was more lovely than the Nereids, or even than Hera herself. The goddesses were, needless to say, rather insulted, and went to Poseidon, god of the sea, to complain. Poseidon promptly sent a sea monster (possibly Cetus?) to ravage the coast. The king and queen were ordered to sacrifice their daughter to appease Poseidon's wrath, and would have done so had Perseus not arrived to kill the monster in the nick of time. As a reward, the hero was wedded to the lovely Andromeda.

By most accounts, Cassiopeia was quite happy with the match. In some versions of the myth, however, the queen objects to the marriage and is turned to stone when Perseus shows her the head of the Gorgon Medusa.

Although she was placed in the heavens by Poseidon the sea-god saw fit to humiliate her one final time (and for all eternity). He placed her so that she is seated on her throne, with her head pointing towards the North Star Polaris. In this position, she spends half of every night upside-down.

27

Centaurus

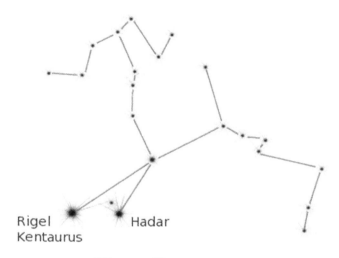

Rigel
Kentaurus   Hadar

THE CENTAUR

Centaurus is one of several constellations that deal with the Labours of Heracles.

In the Fourth Labor, Heracles' assignment was to bring back a rampaging wild boar that was bringing death and destruction to the inhabitants of the northern part of the Peloponnesian peninsula. On his way, he stops to visit a friend of his, a Centaur named Pholus.

Centaurs were half-men, half-horse, who had all descended from Ixion and Nephele (who was in fact a cloud, shaped by Zeus to resemble his wife Hera).

Centaurs were featured in a number of Greek myths, but by and large remained on the periphery of Greek fable.

As Heracles finishes the sumptuous meal provided by Pholus, he then has the effrontery of opening the Centaurs' private wine cask, meant for them alone. The rest of the Centaurs catch the odor of their wine, wafting across hill and dale, and they become enraged.

Gathering up huge boulders, ripping out trees to use as clubs, and arming themselves with axes, the Centaurs advance on the dinner party.

Pholus takes fright, so the battle is left to Heracles. After repulsing a number of Centaurs single-handedly, Heracles then chases the rest of them to the cave of their king, Cheiron.

Heracles shoots an arrow at one fleeing Centaur (Elatus by name), but it passes through his arm and strikes Cheiron on the knee. You may recall that Heracles' arrows were all dipped in poison, so each was fatal, no matter how slight the wound. Cheiron was a great friend of Heracles, and our hero is devastated. He tries to assist Cheiron, but there is nothing to be done.

Cheiron was immortal, so the poison couldn't kill him, only cause great pain that would last through eternity. He descends to the depths of his cave, his screams of agony echoing throughout the cavernous walls.

Eventually Prometheus takes pity on the long-suffering king of the Centaurs, and offers to take over Cheiron's immortality, if Zeus would agree. Zeus does agree, so Cheiron's agony finally comes to an end, and Zeus places the great king of the Centaurs in the heavens.

Back to the previous battle. The Centaur Pholus looks over the dead and dying and wonders how Heracles' arrows could be so fatal. He plucks one arrow out of a body and looks at it, but it slips through his fingers and strikes him on the foot, killing him instantly.

Heracles hears of the tragedy and returns to bury his friend, at the foot of the mountain that bears his name: Mt Pholoe.

This high plateau region in the interior of the peninsula is just up the road from Olympia. Now called Pholois, this is where the Centaur stories of antiquity originated.

It is said that Zeus had held Pholus in very high regard, and therefore also put his likeness in the heavens. Thus the constellation Centaurus represents two Centaurs: Pholus and Cheiron.

The fact that two Centaurs are linked with the constellation is no accident. The earliest extant artifact showing the likeness of a Centaur is a piece of Mycenaean jewellery which shows two centaurs together: half-men, half-horse, facing each other and dancing, similar to satyrs.

These half-men half-horse figures were also transformed at times to half-man half-goat. Many rituals are known to have involved dressing as one of these half-beasts, rituals which may date back to Neolithic times.

Cepheus

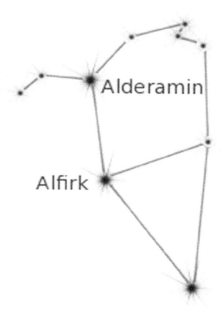

THE KING OF ETHIOPIA

Cepheus, king of Ethiopia, was married to the beautiful Cassiopeia, and together they had a daughter, Andromeda. Although his name is most well-known in connection with his daughter, Cepheus was placed in the sky of his own right: He voyaged as an Argonaut with Jason on the quest for the Golden Fleece.

All three members of the family may be found in the northern sky; Cepheus and Cassiopeia are quite close to the northern celestial pole. Cepheus is generally represented as a robed king with a crown of stars, standing with his left foot planted over the pole and his scepter extended towards his queen.

Cetus

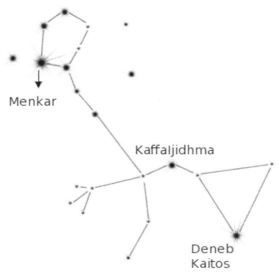

Menkar

Kaffaljidhma

Deneb
Kaitos

THE WHALE

Cetus deserves mention because some say the constellation represents the sea monster sent to Ethiopia as punishment for the boasting of Queen Cassiopeia. The monster nearly kills Andromeda, daughter of Cassiopeia and Cepheus, but is itself killed by the hero Perseus.

More frequently, though, Cetus is represented as a whale, which implies no connection to the Andromeda myth--though it certainly is possible that the ancients perceived whales as monstrous creatures. Either way, the constellation is appropriately a large one, and is relegated to the southern sky--far from Andromeda, Cepheus, and Perseus.

Chamaeleon

beta

alpha

THE CHAMAELEON

Chamaeleon is one of a dozen constellations introduced by Johann Bayer in 1603 for his star atlas Uranometria. Like most of these, Chamaeleon is far to the south. In fact, its stars are circumpolar to residents of the Southern Hemisphere.

Circinus

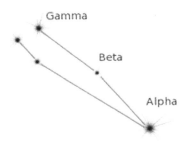

Gamma

Beta

Alpha

THE COMPASS

Circinus, The Compass, is a Southern Hemisphere constellation introduced by Nicolas Louis de Lacaille in the mid-eighteenth century. Only seven Bayer stars are brighter than sixth magnitude.

Columba

Ghusn al Zaitun

Phact

Wezn

THE DOVE

Columba, "The Dove", may refer to the bird the Argonauts sent ahead, to help them pass the narrow strait at the mouth of the Black Sea.

However, early atlas makers called it "Columba Noae", referring to the story of Noah and the Ark, and they depicted the dove carrying an olive branch in its beak.

Coma Berenices

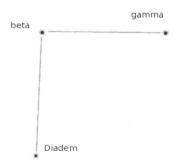

HAIR OF BERENICES

The constellation Coma Berenices refers to a classical story concerning the hair of Berenice, the wife of Ptolemy III of Egypt. While the story is an old one, the constellation is relatively new, being introduced by Tycho Brahe (1546-1601).

According to the story, Ptolemy had waged a long war on the Assyrians, since it was they who had killed his sister. As Ptolemy returned successfully from the war, his wife Berenice had her beautiful tresses ceremoniously clipped and given to Aphrodite, laid out on the temple altar.

As the evening's festivities continued, the shorn hair was discovered to be missing. The priests might be sacrificed, if the queen's hair couldn't be found. It was the astronomer Conon of Samos who came to their rescue - proclaiming that Aphrodite had accepted the gift of Berenice's hair, which now shown brightly in the heavens next to Leo.

Corona Australis

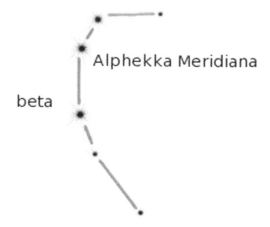

Alphekka Meridiana

beta

THE SOUTHERN CROWN

Corona Australis is a small compact constellation nestled between Sagittarius and Scorpius, just east of Scorpion's stinger.

The constellation is quite old, and is said to represent the crown worn by the centaur Sagittarius (and sometimes known as "Corona Sagittarii").

Corona Borealis

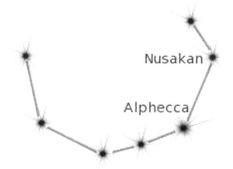

Nusakan

Alphecca

THE NORTHERN CROWN

This constellation is generally associated with Ariadne, the daughter of King Minos of Crete. His wife had borne a hideous monster, half-man and half-bull, and Minos had it shut up in a labyrinth designed by the famous architect Daedalus. The maze was so complex and confusing that Daedalus "was himself scarcely able to find his way back to the entrance" (Metamorphoses VIII 166-167).

Periodically, the Minotaur needed to be fed, and a number of Athenians would be put into the labyrinth for it to eat. This happened twice; on the third feeding, the hero Theseus was one of those chosen as a sacrifice. Ariadne fell in love with him, and offered to help if he would take her away with him when he escaped. He agreed, and she gave him a thread to unwind behind him to mark his passage. He killed the Minotaur, followed the thread out of the labyrinth, and sailed from Crete with Ariadne:

Immediately he set sail for Dia, carrying with him the daughter of Minos; but on the shore of that island he cruelly abandoned his companion. Ariadne, left all alone, was sadly lamenting her fate, when Bacchus put his arms around her, and brought her his aid. He took the crown from her forehead, and set it as a constellation in the sky, to bring her eternal glory. Up through the thin air it soared and, as it flew, its jewels were changed into shining fires. They settled in position, still keeping the appearance of a crown, midway between the kneeling Heracles and Ophiucus, who grasps the snake. (Metamorphoses VIII 174-182).

Corvus

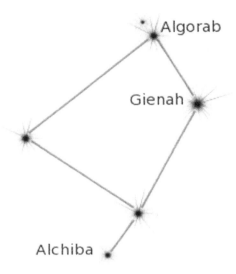

THE CROW

$\mathfrak{C}$orvus, the Crow, was called the Raven by ancient Greeks. The story goes that Apollo sent the raven, or crow, to collect water in the nearby cup ("Crater" = goblet). But the bird wasted its time eating figs. Then, as an excuse for losing time, it gathered up the Water Snake (Hydra) in its claws and flew back, telling Apollo that this creature was the reason for its delay.

Apollo would have none of it, and threw all three: the crow, the goblet, and the water snake, into the heavens. For penance, the crow was made to suffer eternal thirst (and this makes the bird caw raucously instead of sing like normal birds).

Crater

Alkes

GOBLET OF APOLLO

The Crater is the goblet of Apollo. Its shape does resemble a drinking glass, slightly askew in the sky, which is why other ancient cultures also saw this group of stars as some kind of vessel.

 Crux

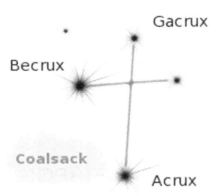

THE SOUTHERN CROSS

Crux, the Southern Cross, is the most familiar constellation in the southern hemisphere. This tiny constellation (the smallest in the entire sky) was once part of Centaurus, but the sight of such a brilliant cross in the sky was so compelling that it became a constellation of its own in the sixteenth century.

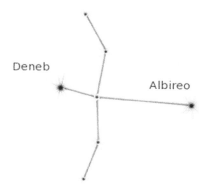

THE SWAN

As is the case with so many of the constellations, there are a number of possible explanations for the presence of the swan in the heavens. Some myths, for instance, state the swan was once the pet of the Queen Cassiopeia. Other versions state that the swan was Cionus, son of Poseidon, who was wrestled to the ground and smothered by Achilles. To save his son, Poseidon immortalized Cionus as a swan.

Another story says the swan is Orpheus, who was murdered by the Thracian women while under the influence of Bacchus. Upon his death, the celebrated musician was placed in the heavens to spend eternity by his harp, Lyra. Yet another variant says that the swan represents the form taken by Zeus when he deceived Leda and fathered Pollux.

According to Ovid, the swan was once Cygnus, son of Sthenele and a close friend of Phaethon. Phaethon died in the river Eridanus after attempting to drive the chariot of the sun, and Cygnus was overcome with grief that Zeus could have struck down his friend:

As he mourned, his voice became thin and shrill, and white feathers hid his hair. His neck grew long, stretching out from his breast, his fingers reddened and a membrane joined them together. Wings clothed his sides, and a blunt beak fastened on his mouth. Cygnus became a new kind of bird: but he put no trust in the skies, or in Zeus, for he remembered how that god had unjustly hurled his flaming bolt. Instead, Cygnus made for marshes and broad lakes, and in his hatred of flames chose to inhabit the rivers, which are the very antithesis of fire (Metamorphoses II 374-382).

Cygnus is easily found in the summer sky. Also called the Northern Cross because of its characteristic shape, its brightest star is Deneb, which is part of the Summer Triangle with Vega and Altair. Cygnus is located next to Cepheus and Lyra.

Delphinus

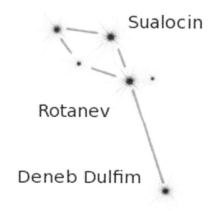

Sualocin

Rotanev

Deneb Dulfim

THE DOLPHIN

Delphinus, "The Dolphin", is an ancient constellation located just west of Pegasus.

Some references name a certain "Arion" as the inspiration for the constellation.

There were two Arions in antiquity. One was a (mythic?) poet who may have lived in the eighth century BC. This Arion, traveling from Sicily to Corinth, was thrown overboard by the ship's crew, eager for the valuables he was carrying. A dolphin is said to have rescued the poet. But this dolphin probably isn't the constellation's origin.

The second Arion was a son of Poseidon and Demeter, and was in fact a horse (like his half-brother Pegasus). Instead of hooves, he had feet on his right side. And, unlike most horses, he could talk. But this Arion also has nothing to do with the constellation.

It is most likely however that the constellation is associated with Poseidon. It was probably his way of thanking one of his messengers for a job well done.

As God of the Sea, Poseidon had fifty sea-nymphs at his court. These were all born of Nereus and known therefore as the Nereids.

While Poseidon had many casual love affairs, when he set out to find a wife he was concerned that she be accustomed to life in the sea. His first choice was Thetis, one of the fifty Nereids. But he learned that any son born of Thetis would grow to become greater than his father. Clearly Poseidon couldn't accept that prophecy.

As a side note, Thetis married Peleus, a mortal, and they had a famous son named Achilles. Thetis dipped Achilles in the river Styx to make him invulnerable to his enemies. As most people now knows, since his mother grasped him by the heels, they were the only part of Achilles which were vulnerable. Wouldn't you know, the day would come when he'd get a poisoned arrow in his heel and die from it.

Poseidon's next choice in marriage was a sister of Thetis, called Amphitrite. But when Poseidon pressed Amphitrite to marry him, she was quite disgusted by the thought and fled to the far-off Atlas Mountains. Poseidon sent a number of messengers to persuade her to return, as his wife, to his underwater realm.

The messenger who succeeded in this task was the

dolphin Delphinus. Amphitrite was so beguiled by Delphinus' pleadings she relented and returned to Poseidon and became the Queen of the Sea. They had many children.

Delphinus was later put in the heavens as a constellation by a grateful Poseidon.

The asterism is rather curious, for its four main stars form a rectangle called "Job's Coffin". This is probably a hang-over from the time Delphinus was interpreted as a whale, as in Chapter 41 of Job where God challenged Job: "Canst thou draw out leviathan with an hook?" However there is no reference to Job being swallowed by a whale, as happened with Jonah, so the name Job's Coffin remains a bit of a mystery.

Dorado

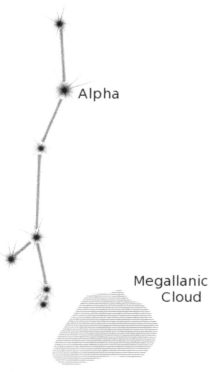

Alpha

Megallanic
Cloud

THE GOLDFISH

$\mathfrak{D}$orado was introduced by Johann Bayer in 1603 in his epoch-making star atlas, Uranometria.

Dorado, "The Goldfish", is also known as "The Swordfish". While the Bayer stars are not very bright, there are several objects of interest in the constellation, notably the Large Magellanic Cloud and the Tarantula Nebula.

Draco

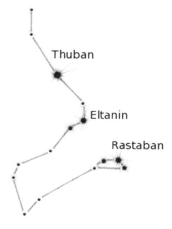

Thuban

Eltanin

Rastaban

THE DRAGON

It is unclear precisely which mythological dragon Draco represents. There are, however, three main contenders.

One version--the least likely--of the Draco story is that the dragon fought Minerva during the wars between the giants and the gods. Minerva threw Draco's twisted body into the heavens before it had time to unwind itself.

Another possibility is that Draco represents the dragon who guarded the golden apples in the garden of the Hesperides. One of the labors of Heracles was to steal these apples (some sources state it was his eleventh labor, others it was his twelfth). This was, according to Bulfinch, the most difficult labor of all..., for Heracles did not know where to find them. These were the apples which Hera had received at her wedding from the goddess of the Earth, and which she had entrusted to the keeping of the daughters of Hesperus, assisted by a watchful dragon. After various adventures, Heracles arrived at Mount Atlas in Africa. Atlas was one of the Titans who had warred against the gods, and after they were subdued, Atlas was condemned to bear on his shoulders the weight of the heavens. He was the father of the Hesperides, and Heracles thought might, if any one could, find the apples and bring them to him (Bulfinch's Mythology, 136).

Heracles suggested this plan to Atlas, who pointed out two problems: first, he could not simply drop his burden; second, there was the awful guardian dragon. Heracles responded by throwing his spear into the garden of the Hesperides and killing the hundred-headed beast, and then taking the burden on his own shoulders. Atlas retrieved the apples and, reluctantly taking the burden onto his shoulders once again, gave them to Heracles. Hera placed the dragon in the heavens as a reward for his faithful service.

By far the most commonly accepted version of Draco's arrival in the heavens, however, is that Draco was the dragon killed by Cadmus. Cadmus was the brother of Europa, who was carried off to Crete by Zeus in the form of a bull (Taurus). Cadmus was ordered by his father to go in search of his sister, and told he could not return unless he brought Europa back with him. "Cadmus wandered over the whole world: for who can lay hands on what Jove has stolen away? Driven to avoid his native country and his father's wrath, he made a pilgrimage to Apollo's oracle, and begged him to say what land he should dwell in" (Metamorphoses III 9-11).

Cadmus followed Apollo's advice and found a suitable site for his new city. He sent his attendants to find fresh water to offer as a libation to Zeus, and they wandered into a cave with springs. As they were getting water, however, they were all killed by "the serpent of Mars, a creature with a wonderful golden crest; fire flashed from its eyes, its body was all puffed up from poison, and from its mouth, set with a triple row of teeth, flickered a three-forked tongue" (Metamorphoses III 31-34). After his companions did not return, Cadmus himself went into the cave and discovered the dragon. He killed it with his spear, and then (upon the order of Minerva) sowed the dragon's teeth in the ground. From the teeth sprung warriors, who battled each other until only five were left. These five, along with Cadmus himself, were the first people of the city of Thebes.

It is interesting, however, to note that Ovid himself does not equate the dragon of Mars with Draco. In fact, in book III of Metamorphoses, he describes the dragon killed by Cadmus in terms of the constellation: "It was as huge as the Serpent that twines between the two Bears in the sky, if its full length were seen uncoiled" (45-47).

The Serpent described by Ovid is certainly the same one as we see today, twisting past Cepheus and between Ursa Major and Ursa Minor in the north, with its head beneath the foot of Heracles. Its location therefore seems to fit best with the myth that Draco was the dragon in the garden of the Hesperides.

Equuleus

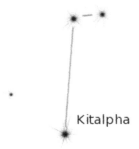

Pherasauval

Kitalpha

THE LITTLE HORSE

Equuleus, "The Little Horse", is one of the smallest constellations in the heavens. It's quite old, and may have been founded by Ptolemy in the second century AD. However the author of the Almagest often borrowed from others and it is possible his principal source, Hipparchus, was the true creator of this constellation.

The outstanding Greek astronomer Hipparchus (fl 146-127 BC) composed the first star catalog, of about 850 stars. He also discovered the precession of the equinoxes and invented trigonometry. It is not known if he actually created any constellations.

The "little horse" that the name refers to is lost in antiquity. Some sources believe it to be a half-brother of Pegasus, Celeris. However I've not found any reference to this character. The only brother of Pegasus that I've come across is Chrysaor, born simultaneously with Pegasus. Instead of a horse, Chrysaor was a warrior.

Eridanus

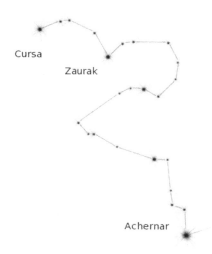

Cursa

Zaurak

Achernar

THE RIVER

Eridanus is a river in northern Italy, now known as the River Po. Called by Virgil the "king of rivers," Eridanus was made famous in connection with the death of Phaethon.

Phaethon was the son of Phoebus Apollo and the nymph Clymene. For his birthday one year, Phaethon asked his father for some proof that he was indeed the son of the sun-god. Apollo said he would give the boy any gift he desired as a token of his fatherly love, and Phaethon promptly asked for the chance to drive the chariot of the sun. His father balked, knowing that no mortal youth could possibly have the strength necessary to control the horses. However, Phaethon insisted, and Apollo had granted his word.

Phaethon drove off on the route of the sun, but sure enough, he could not control the powerful horses. He drove too close to the heavens, and then plunged too close to the earth, scorching both realms. Gaia endured the sun's heat until she could bear it no more, and then she called upon Zeus for help:

The omnipotent father called upon the gods and even upon the sun himself, who had bestowed his car upon Phaethon, to be his witnesses that, if he did not bring help, the whole world would come to a grievous end. Then he mounted up to the highest point of heaven, that height from which he is wont to spread clouds over the broad lands of earth, whence he sends forth his thunderings and hurls his flashing bolts: he had no clouds then to draw over the world, no rain to shower down from the skies. He sent forth a thunderclap and, poising his bolt close by his right ear, launched it against the charioteer....Phaethon, with flames searing his glowing locks, was flung headlong, and went hurtling down through the air, leaving a long trail behind: just as a star, though it does not really fall, could yet be thought to fall from a clear sky. Far from his native land, in a distant part of the world, the river Eridanus received him, and bathed his charred features" (Metamorphoses II 304-327).

As a constellation, Eridanus is the longest in the sky, meandering from Orion to Cetus.

Fornax

Fornacis

THE FURNACE

Fornax, "The Furnace", is another of those constellations created by Nicolas Louis de Lacaille in the mid-eighteenth century; he took several dozen fairly bright stars away from the middle of Eridanus and called the result Fornax Chemica.

Gemini

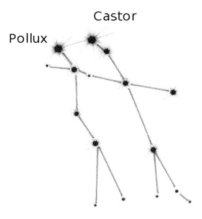

Pollux · Castor

THE TWINS

Gemini is a zodiacal constellation representing the twin brothers Castor and Pollux. Both were mothered by Leda, and were therefore brothers of Helen, but they had different fathers: In one night, Leda was made pregnant both by Zeus in the form of a swan and by her husband, the king Tyndarus of Sparta. Pollux, as the son of a god, was immortal and was renowned for his strength, while his mortal brother Castor was famous for his skill with horses. Both brothers voyaged in search of the Golden Fleece as Argonauts, and then fought in the Trojan War to bring their sister home to her husband Menelaus. They are traditionally depicted as armed with spears and riding a matched pair of snow-white horses.

The most common explanation for their presence in the heavens is that Pollux was overcome with sorrow when his mortal brother died, and begged Zeus to allow him to share his immortality. Zeus, acknowledging the heroism of both brothers, consented and reunited the pair in the heavens.

Grus

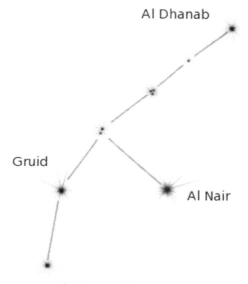

Al Dhanab

Gruid

Al Nair

THE CRANE

Grus lies just below Piscis Austrinus, and at one time was part of that constellation. Grus (The Crane) was so named by Johann Bayer, as listed in his 1603 star atlas.

The constellation is replete with very faint spiral galaxies, from eleventh to thirteenth magnitude, and a number of fine binaries, but little else.

Heracles

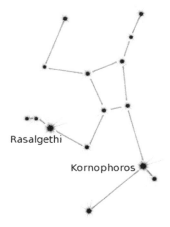

Rasalgethi

Kornophoros

$\mathfrak{H}$eracles was perhaps the greatest hero in all mythology. He was the son of Zeus and Alcmena, and was hounded all his life by Hera. (This is deliciously ironic, because in the original Greek myths, Hera is named Hera and Heracles is Heracles, which means "glory of Hera.") Hera was unhappy with Zeus's infidelity, and saw Heracles as a living, breathing symbol of her shame. She delayed his birth, and when Heracles was a mere baby (but a big one!) sent two snakes into the crib he shared with his mortal half-twin Iphicles. Heracles killed them both with his bare hands, marking the beginning of his career as a monster-killer.

After a precocious childhood and adolesence, Heracles married Megara (daughter of Creon, king of Thebes). Hera succeeded in driving him mad, though, and he killed his wife and his children. As atonement, he serves the king Eurystheus, performing the twelve labors for which he is most famed:

1. He wrestled and killed the Nemean Lion (Leo) in its den, then used one of the beast's teeth to remove the otherwise impenetrable hide. He wore the hide as protection from then on.

2. He killed the Lernaean Hydra, a poisonous monster which could regenerate its heads, growing two each time one was lopped off. Heracles managed this by burning the stump of each before anything could grow back and burying the one immortal head beneath a rock. While battling the Hydra, his feet were nipped by a crab sent by Hera.

3. He captured the Cerynean Hind, a stag with golden horns which was famous for its speed, after a year-long pursuit.

4. He captured the Erymanthian Boar and killed the centaurs Pholus and Chiron who opposed him.

5. He successfully cleaned the Augean Stables, which had held 3000 oxen for thirty years without ever having been cleaned, in one night by redirecting the rivers Alpheus and Peneus through them.

6. He killed the Stymphalian Birds, which fed on human flesh in Arcadia.

7. He captured the Cretan Bull.

8. He captured the mares of Diomedes, which fed on human flesh, by feeding them their owner.

9. He stole the girdle of Hippolyta, queen of the Amazons.

10. He stole the man-eating cattle of Geryon.

11. He stole the three-headed guard dog Cerberus from the underworld.

12. He obtained the golden apples of the Hesperides, killing a dragon to do so.

Heracles also accompanied Jason on his quest for the Golden Fleece and assisted in the war between the gods and the giants. He remarried, and eventually died after accidentally poisoned by his wife Deineira. He was subsequently immortalized, even though he was by birth only half immortal..

Horologium

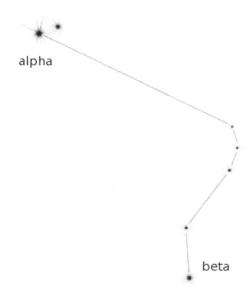

alpha

beta

THE CLOCK

It was created in the 18th century by Abbé Nicolas Louis de Lacaille, who originally named it **Horologium Oscillitorium** after the pendulum clock to honour its inventor, Christiaan Huygens. The name has since been shortened to be less cumbersome.

Hydra

Alphard

THE WATER-SNAKE

This constellation represents the Lernaean Hydra, slain by Heracles as his second labor. The Hydra was a multi-headed monster--according to Diodorus (first century B.C.), it had a hundred heads; Simonides (sixth century B.C.) said it had fifty. The most common opinion, however, seems to be that it had nine. What made the Hydra so difficult was the fact that, whenever one of its heads was chopped off, two would grow in its place. Heracles managed to get around this rather major obstacle by having his nephew, Iolaus, cauterize each stump with a hot iron as soon as Heracles could chop off a head. The hero then buried the monster's immortal head beneath a rock. The task was made somewhat more difficult by Hera, who sent a crab to nip at the feet of Heracles while he battled the Hydra.

Hydra is a long and wandering constellation, stretching almost from Canis Minor to Libra. It lies south of Cancer, Leo, and Virgo, and is best seen in the northern hemisphere during the months of February through May.

Hydrus

Alpha

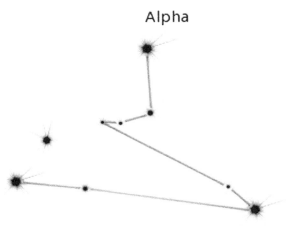

THE LESSER SNAKE

Hydrus, "The Lesser Snake", was one of Johann Bayer's constellations, found first in his 1603 publication Uranometria. It was meant to be the southern hemisphere's answer to Hydra, but it has far fewer objects of interest.

Hydrus is a rather stiff snake, perhaps mostly resembling a cobra, with its head erect and body curled. As with most of these obscure constellations, its Bayer stars are far from complete, and fairly faint.

Indus

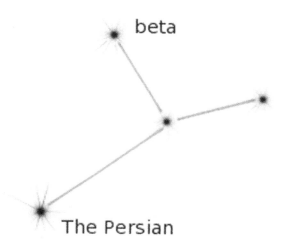

beta

The Persian

Johann Bayer wanted to honour the American Indian in his collection of new constellations for his 1603 book Uranometria.

Lacerta

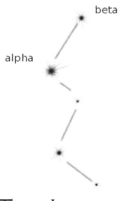

beta

alpha

THE LIZARD

Lacerta, is one of seven constellations introduced by Johannes Hevelius.

Born in Gdansk, Poland, 28 January 1611, Hevelius died the same day in the same place 76 years later.

Hevelius is mostly known for his atlas of the Moon (Selenographia, 1647). His star catalog of 1564 stars was the most complete up to that time. It was in this catalog and an accompanying celestial atlas (Prodromus Astronomiae), both published posthumously in 1690, that Hevelius introduced seven new constellations.

Hevelius had built his own observatory, on the roof of his house, as well as a number of quality telescopes. His stellar observations were the most accurate to his time, and for that reason the celestial atlas was a remarkable achievement.

Leo

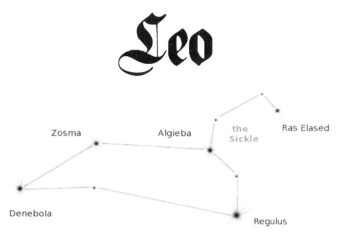

Zosma   Algieba   the Sickle   Ras Elased

Denebola

Regulus

THE LION

Leo is generally accepted to represent the Nemean Lion, killed by Heracles during his first labor. According to myth, the Nemean lion had an impenetrable skin. Heracles got around this potentially serious obstacle by wrestling the lion and strangling it to death. He then removed one of its claws, and used it to skin the animal. From then on, Heracles wore the skin of the Nemean Lion as protection.

Leo is easy to locate; following the pointer stars of the Big Dipper south approximates the location of the bright blue-white star Regulus in Leo's chest.

Leo Minor

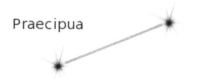

Praecipua

LESSER LION

Leo Minor is one of the seven constellations introduced by Johannes Hevelius in his posthumous catalog of 1690. The others he introduced are Canes Venatici, Lacerta, Lynx, Scutum, Sextans, and Vulpecula.

Lepus

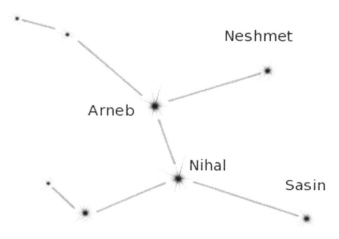

Neshmet

Arneb

Nihal

Sasin

THE HARE

Lepus, "The Hare", is an ancient constellation found under the feet of Orion, the Hunter. No one seems to know just which culture first saw the constellation as an animal; the Arabs saw it as the "throne of the central one" (i.e. Orion).

Lepus, The Hare is not to be confused with Lupus, The Wolf, which is a spring constellation.

Lepus is often ignored, as Orion is such a dominating constellation. Yet Lepus contains a number of interesting objects. Its Bayer stars are generally third and fourth magnitude.

Libra

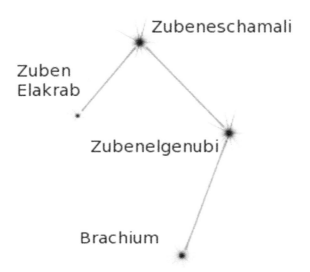

Zubeneschamali

Zuben
Elakrab

Zubenelgenubi

Brachium

THE SCALES

Libra is a zodiacal constellation. It represents the balance or scales, and is one of the oldest constellations. Although now associated with Virgo, a goddess of justice who had scales as the emblem of her office, it was once associated with the fall equinox. On that day, the days and nights are of equal length (i.e. the moon and the sun are in balance).

Libra is represented in the heavens next to the hand of Virgo.

Lupus

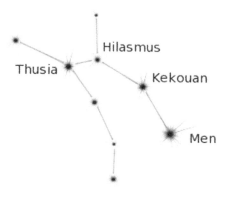

Thusia
Hilasmus
Kekouan
Men

THE WOLF

The constellation may refer to the ancient king of Arcadia, King Lycaon (a word which is related to both 'wolf' and 'light').

King Lycaon, who ruled Arcadia with his fifty sons, was said to continue the practice of human sacrifice when other parts of Greece had abolished it as barbaric.

One variation of the story has King Lycaon offering Zeus the sacrifice of a young boy, which angered Zeus so much he promptly changed Lycaon into a wolf and struck his house down with lightning, killing all his fifty sons.

In another version Zeus one day visited Arcadia disguised as a simple traveller. Lycaon and his sons offered him soup made not only from the meat of goats and sheep, but also of his own son Nyctimus. Zeus overthrew the table in disgust and killed all the king's sons with lightning bolts (restoring the life of Nyctimus in the process).

Lynx

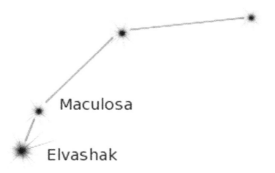

Alsciaukat

Maculosa

Elvashak

The name Lynx never stood for the animal itself. Hevelius, who invented the constellation, said anyone who wanted to study the stars here should have eyes like a lynx.

As with many other minor constellations invented by Hevelius and others to fill in the blanks, Lynx is nothing more than a bumpy line running south from 2 Lyncis down to alpha Lyncis, which sits just north of the border of Leo with Cancer.

Actually when you connect the stars, the figure of a giant seagull comes to mind, or an albatross perhaps.

Lyra

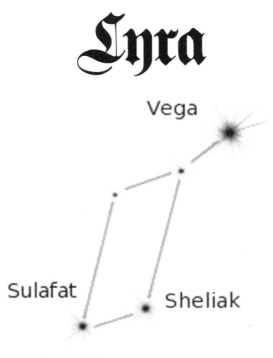

Vega

Sulafat Sheliak

THE LYRE

Lyra represents the lyre played by Orpheus, musician of the Argonauts and son of Apollo and the muse Calliope. Apollo gave his son the lyre as a gift, and Orpheus played it so well that even the wild beasts, the rocks, and the trees were charmed by his music. He fell deeply in love with the nymph Eurydice, and the two were married. Their wedded bliss did not last for very long, however. Eurydice was wandering in the fields with some other nymphs when she was seen by the shepherd Aristaeus. Aristaeus was struck by her beauty and pursued her; as she fled, she was bitten by a snake in the grass and died of the serpent's poison.

Orpheus was devastated. He decided to seek out his wife in the underworld, and gained an audience with Pluto and Persephone. The king and queen of the underworld, like

71

all others, were charmed by his music and granted him permission to take Eurydice back to the land of the living with him:

They called Eurydice. She was among the ghosts who had but newly come, and walked slowly because of her injury. Thracian Orpheus received her, but on condition that he must not look back until he had emerged from the valleys of Avernus or else the gift he had been given would be taken from him.

Up the sloping path, through the mute silence they made their way, up the steep dark track, wrapped in impenetrable gloom, till they had almost reached the surface of the earth. Here, anxious in case his wife's strength be failing and eager to see her, the lover looked behind him, and straightaway Eurydice slipped back into the depths. Orpheus stretched out his arms, straining to clasp her and be clasped; but the hapless man touched nothing but yielding air. Eurydice, dying now a second time, uttered no complaint against her husband. What was there to complain of, that she had been loved? With a last farewell which scarcely reached his ears, she fell back again into the same place from which she had come (Metamorphoses X 47-63).

According to Ovid, Orpheus was so heartbroken from having lost his love not once, but twice, that he rejected the company of women in favor of that of small boys. The women of Thrace were infuriated and, while maddened during Bacchic rites, hurled rocks at the bard. The rocks, tamed by the sound of Orpheus's lyre, at first fell harmlessly at his feet, but the shrieks of the infuriated women soon drowned out the music. The women dismembered Orpheus, throwing his lyre and his head into the river Hebrus. The Muses gathered up his limbs and buried them, and Orpheus went to the underworld to spend eternity with Eurydice. Zeus himself cast the bard's lyre into the sky.

Mensa

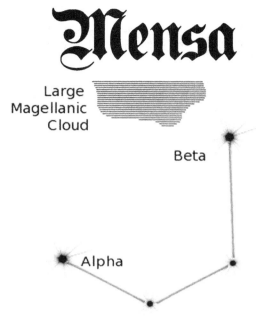

Large Magellanic Cloud

Beta

Alpha

THE TABLE

Mensa, The Table, is another of Nicolas de Lacaille's creations, this one named for the Table Mountain at the Cape of Good Hope, where Lacaille observed the southern hemisphere skies in the mid eighteenth century.

The asterism shows an upside down mountain top. The mountain is seen right-side up in the Southern Hemisphere around midnight in mid-July.

Microscopium

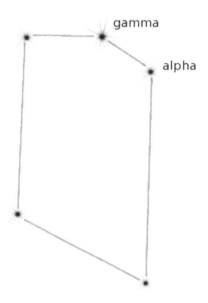

gamma

alpha

THE MICROSCOPE

Microscopium, The Microscope, is one of Nicolas de Lacaille's creations, celebrating yet another scientific instrument.

𝔐onoceros

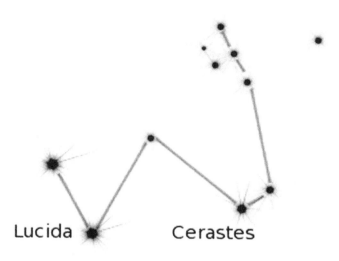

Lucida   Cerastes

THE UNICORN

𝔉lanked by Orion and Canis Minor, with Gemini above and Canis Major below, the faint constellation Monoceros ("the Unicorn") is often overlooked.

While the constellation may have been in existence prior to the seventeenth century, its first historical reference appears in Jakob Bartsch's star chart of 1624, under the name "Unicornu". It is believed that Bartsch (who incidentally was Johannes Kepler's son-in-law) relied on earlier works, but such works have never been identified.

It takes a lot of imagination to fashion a unicorn out of this group of stars. In fact, there are several variations.

Musca

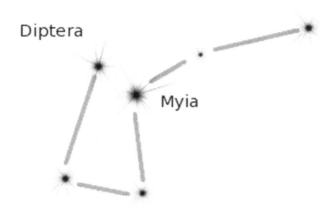

THE FLY

Musca, "The Fly", is a southern hemisphere constellation introduced by Johann Bayer. He called it Apis, "The Bee"; perhaps because of its similarity with "Apus", this name didn't stick.

The full name is actually Musca Australis vel Indica (The Southern or Indian Fly), which distinguished it from the now obsolete Musca Borealis, the Northern Fly.

Norma

theta

epsilon

gamma 2

THE LEVEL

Norma is another of those relatively insignificant constellations in the Southern Hemisphere. Invented by Nicolas Louis de Lacaille in the mid-eighteenth century, the constellation represents a scientific instrument, "the level". The original name was "Norma et Regula" (the level and the square).

Octans

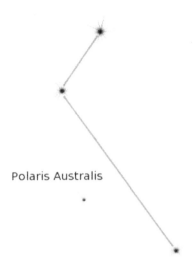

Polaris Australis

Octans is a rather non-descript constellation which includes the southern polar region. The constellation was devised by Nicolas Louis de Lacaille in 1752. It commemorates the octant, which was invented by John Hadley in 1730. In fact the full name of the constellation is "Octans Hadleianus".

The instrument divided the circle into eight parts, which facilitated the making of angular measurements in both astronomy and navigation.

Ophiuchus

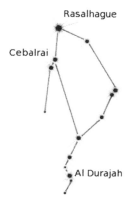

There is some disagreement over the origin of this constellation. Apparently it was once known as Asclepius, who was the Greek god of medicine. One such reference was made in the writings of Eudoxus, in the fourth century BC.

Eudoxus (c400-c347 BC) deserves to be better known. He may have been a member of Plato's Academy, and it is possible he was its head for some time.

Eudoxus was a prolific writer of scientific subjects, and thinkers such as Euclid incorporated much of his work into their own. He mapped out the constellations, and the result became the main star reference for hundreds of years. Among other feats, he divided the sky into degrees of longitude and latitude and devised a better calendar. He was also a well known geographer and mathematician, but it was his work on astronomy that he is principally remembered.

Later Greek stories arose about Carnabon, a king of the Getae, who killed a famous dragon, or even of Heracles, who (you might recall) killed Draco. Thus the story of the man and serpent came to represent a host of individuals, but most authorities now seem to opt for Asclepius, or Aesculapius, which is the Latin equivalent of the Greek god of medicine.

Son of Apollo and a nymph called Coronis, Asclepius was taught medicine by the centaur Chiron. (His mythology also arises from Thessaly, where the stories of the centaurs originated.)

Asclepius became the Argonauts' surgeon, sailing with them on the ship Argo, and he managed to bring back to life a number of people, including the son of King Minos of Crete.

It was after Asclepius tried to revive Orion, bitten by the scorpion, that Pluto began to complain. He argued to Zeus that if Asclepius had his way he would rob Pluto of the entire population of Hades. Zeus agreed; they couldn't permit men to be immortal. So he sent a thunderbolt to end Asclepius's life.

Zeus later put Asclepius in the heavens along with the Serpent. The serpent has long been a symbol for renewed life.

While the cult of Asclepius began in Thessaly, temples were built throughout Greece, especially near healing springs. Around 300 BC the cult arrived in Rome.

Ancient sculpture typically shows the god bare breasted, attired in a long flowing cloak, and holding a staff with a serpent coiled about it. This is perhaps the forerunner of the modern medical symbol of the caduceus.

Orion

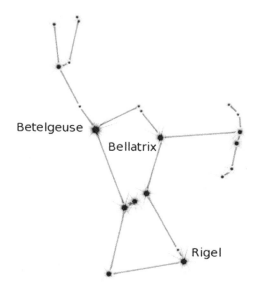

Betelgeuse

Bellatrix

Rigel

THE HUNTER

There are two different versions of the Orion myth, depending on the identity of his parents. The first of these identifies the sea-god Poseidon as Orion's father and the great huntress Queen Euryale of the Amazons as his mother. Orion inherited her talent, and became the greatest hunter in the world. Unfortunately for him, with his immense strength came an immense ego, and he boasted that he could best any animal on earth. In response to his vanity, a single small scorpion stung him and killed him.

Another version of the Orion myth states that he had no mother but was a gift to a pious peasant from Zeus, Poseidon, and Hermes. "Orion supposedly was able to walk on water and had greater strength and stature than any other mortal. A skilled blacksmith, he fabricated a subterranean palace for Hephaestus. He also walled in the coasts of Sicily against the encroaching sea and built a temple to the gods there" (Magee, 48). Orion fell in love with Merope, daughter of Oenopion and princess of Chios. Her father the king, however, would not consent to give Orion his daughter's hand in marriage--even after the hunter rid their island of wild beasts. In anger,

Orion attempted to gain possession of the maiden by violence. Her father, incensed at this conduct, having made Orion drunk, deprived him of his sight and cast him out on the seashore. The blinded hero followed the sound of a Cyclops' hammer till he reached Lemnos, and came to the forge of Vulcan, who, taking pity on him, gave him Kedalion, one of his men, to be his guide to the abode of the sun. Placing Kedalion on his shoulders, Orion proceeded to the east, and there meeting the sun-god, was restored to sight by his beam.

After this he dwelt as a hunter with Artemis, with whom he was a favorite, and it is even said she was about to marry him. Her brother [Apollo] was highly displeased and child her [she was, after all, a virgin huntress], but to no purpose. One day, observing Orion wading through the ocean with his head just above the water, Apollo pointed it out to his sister and maintained that she could not hit that black thing on the sea. The archer-goddess discharged a shaft with fatal aim. The waves rolled the body of Orion to the land, and bewailing her fatal error with many tears, Artemis placed him among the stars (Bulfinch's Mythology, 191-192).

It is also stated in some versions that Apollo, worried for Artemis' chastity, sent a scorpion to kill Orion.

Pavo

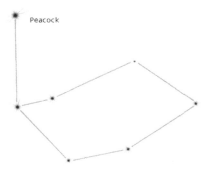

Peacock

THE PEACOCK

$\mathfrak{H}$era, wife of Zeus and hence the Queen of the heavens, was an excessively jealous wife. And with good reason; Zeus was excessively amorous. Scholars have assiduously traced at least fifty lovers and mistresses of this supreme Greek god. Io was one of these lovers.

The trouble was, Io was one of Hera's priestesses, and Hera soon discovered the infidelity. To protect Io, Zeus transformed her into a heifer. But Hera was not fooled, and she claimed ownership over the heifer, then chose Argus Panoptes to guard the animal.

As indicated by its name, Argus Panoptes was "all eyes". Indeed, the beast had one hundred eyes, which surely should have been sufficient to guard one small heifer.

Zeus engaged Hermes with the task of rescuing Io. To avoid detection by one of Argus' one hundred eyes, Hermes charmed the animal with a flute when it was fast asleep, then threw a huge boulder on top of it, and for good measure cut off its head.

An angry Hera set a gadfly to pester Io, who then roamed around most of the Mediterranean nations before finally settling down in Egypt, where Zeus changed her back into human form. She later established the worship of Isis in Egypt.

As for the unfortunate Argus Panoptes, Hera put all of its many eyes on the tail of her sacred bird, the peacock. Only much later, in the seventeenth century, would the peacock itself become part of the heavenly zoo. Johann Bayer introduced the constellation in Uranometria in 1603, along with a number of other birds: Apus, Grus, Phoenix, and Tucana.

Pavo is a large constellation showing the tail of the peacock in full display. While the Bayer stars are not very bright, there are several deep sky objects of interest in the constellation.

Pegasus

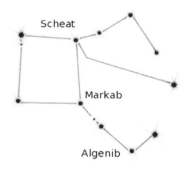

Scheat

Markab

Algenib

THE WINGED HORSE

Pegasus, the winged horse, flew out of the head of Medusa when Perseus slew her. It was fathered by Poseidon, some time earlier, and waited for the Gorgon's death to appear. (Medusa's story is told under the constellation "Cepheus".)

Athene gave Pegasus to Bellerophon (a grandson of Sisyphus), who used the winged creature in his fight against the Chimaera - a monstrous female with three heads.

Bellerophon shot arrows at the beast as he flew above her on Pegasus, then he stuck between her jaws a huge lump of lead. The monster's own breath melted the lead, which then flowed down her throat and burned her to death.

Now Bellerophon was sent off on another mission, which he accomplished with equal aplomb. Flushed with victory, he flew off for Olympus, home of the gods, as if he too were immortal. Zeus sent a gadfly, which stung Pegasus on the bum, and Bellerophon was kicked off the horse.

Pegasus went alone to Olympus, where he was used by Zeus to carry around his thunderbolts. As for Bellerophon, for his presumption of greatness, he wandered about the earth for the rest of his life, blind, lame, and shunned by man, until dying of old age.

Pegasus is a conspicuous constellation which includes the so-called "Great Square of Pegasus". However it must now share the northeast corner of the square with Andromeda: delta Pegasus was given to Andromeda, to provide the lady with a head!

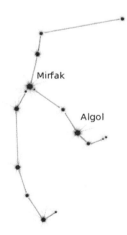

Perseus was one of the great heroes of classical mythology. He was the son of Zeus and Danae, and is best known for his killing of the Gorgon Medusa. This was a rather complex task, as anyone who saw her hideous face would be turned immediately to stone--the Gorgons, according to Bulfinch, were "monstrous females with huge teeth like those of swine, brazen claws, and snaky hair" (Bulfinch's Mythology, 109). Perseus accomplishes it, however, by the aid of Pluto, Mercury and Minerva. Pluto lent his helmet of invisibility to Perseus, Mercury lent the hero his winged sandals, and Minerva allowed him the use of her shield. With the aid of the helmet and the sandals, Perseus was able to get within striking range without being detected by Medusa or the two immortal Gorgons. He then used the reflection on the shield to guide his killing blow, and flew off unharmed bearing the head of Medusa:

He was bringing back the Gorgon's head, the memorable trophy he had won in his contest with that snaky-haired monster. As the victorious hero hovered over Libya's desert sands, drops of blood fell from the head. The earth caught them as they fell, and changed them into snakes of different kinds. So it came about that that land is full of deadly serpents. Thereafter, Perseus was driven by warring winds all over the vast expanse of sky: like a raincloud, he was blown this way and that. He flew over the whole earth, looking down from the heights of heaven to the land which lay far below (Metamorphoses IV 615-624).

He was rather tired and wanted to rest when he arrived at the lands of Atlas, at the ends of the earth. Atlas, however, tried to turn him away with his considerably greater strength. Perseus was infuriated and showed him the head of Medusa, turning the Titan into "a mountain as huge as the giant he had been. His beard and hair were turned into trees, his hands and shoulders were mountain ridges, and what had been his head was now the mountain top. His bones became rock. Then, expanding in all directions, he increased to a tremendous size--such was the will of the gods--and the whole sky with its many stars rested upon him" (Metamorphoses IV 656-662). Perseus flew on until he spotted the beautiful maiden Andromeda, who was chained to the rocky shore as a sacrifice to a sea monster. Perseus promptly fell in love with her, killed the monster, and married the princess.

There are some variants on the myth of Perseus. According to some versions, he had to win the winged sandals and the helmet from the three Graeae, sisters of the Gorgons who shared one eye and one tooth among them. He stole the eye and the tooth, returning them only in exchange for the sandals and the helmet he needed to defeat Medusa.

When he died many years later, Perseus was immortalized as a constellation. He may be found near Andromeda and her parents, Cepheus and Cassiopeia, in the northern sky. The hero is depicted with a sword in one hand and the head of Medusa in the other; it is interesting to note the the eye of Medusa is the star Algol. Algol, which means "Demon Star" in Arabic, is an eclipsing binary star--it is normally about as bright as Polaris (second magnitude), but every two and a half days it becomes dimmer for roughly eight hours as the dimmer star of the pair passes between the brighter and the earth.

Phoenix

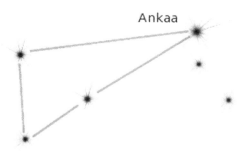

Ankaa

Phoenix, the mythical bird rising from its own ashes, is another of those Southern Hemisphere constellations introduced by Johann Bayer in 1603.

In the past the constellation had been known as "The Boat" by the Arabs, then it became an eagle or other type of bird, so Bayer's decision to call it a phoenix does have some vague precedence.

Pictor

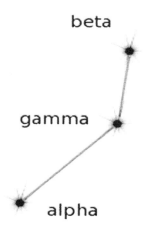

beta

gamma

alpha

THE EASEL

Pictor, "The Painter's Easel", is an invention of Nicolas Louis de Lacaille, who originally called the constellation "Le Chevalet et la Palette" (The Painter's Easel and Palette).

Pisces

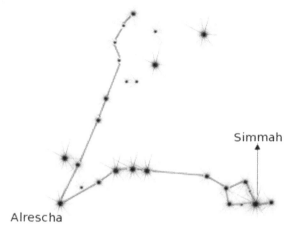

Simmah

Alrescha

THE FISH

The horrible earthborn giant Typhoeus suddenly appeared one day, startling all the gods into taking on different forms to flee. Zues, for instance, transformed himself into a ram; Hermes became an ibis; Apollo took on the shape of a crow; Artemis hid herself as a cat; and Bacchus disguised himself as a goat. Aphrodite and her son Eros were bathing on the banks of the Euphrates River that day, and took on the shapes of a pair of fish to escape danger. Minerva later immortalized the event by placing the figures of two fish amongst the stars.

The zodiacal constellation Pisces represents two fish, tied together with a cord. The constellation is neither particularly bright nor easy to locate, but it lies near Pegasus and Aquarius.

Piscis Austrinus

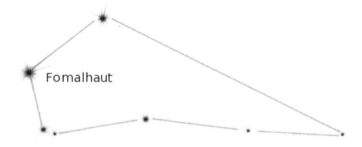

Fomalhaut

THE LARGE SOUTHERN FISH

Piscis Austrinus, also known as Piscis Australis, is a fish lying on its back, drinking in the waters pouring from the jars of Aquarius. The asterism leaves a lot to the imagination.

The constellation was known in ancient times, and is said to be the original "Pisces". It is thought that the constellation referred to the Assyrian fish god Dagon and the Babylonian god Oannes. Even the Arabs called the constellation Al Hut al Janubiyy (The Large Southern Fish).

The bright star Fomalhaut (alpha PsA) was so named from Fum al Hut, meaning "The Fish's Mouth", although it carried many other names as well, including Al Difdi al Awwal ("The First Frog").

Puppis

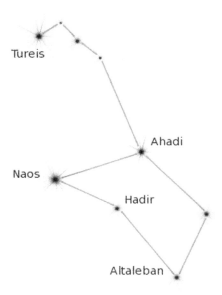

THE STERN

Puppis, "The Stern", is the largest constellation associated with the former constellation "Argo Navis", the Argonauts' Ship.

It was Nicolas Louis de Lacaille who dismantled the older constellation in the mid-eighteenth century, breaking it into four smaller constellations: Carina, Pyxis, Puppis, and Vela.

Not only quite large, the constellation spans a rich area of the Milky Way, guaranteeing the amateur astronomer a number of fine objects to study.

Pyxis

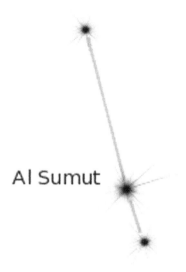

Al Sumut

THE COMPASS

Pyxis, "The Compass", is one of Nicolas Louis de Lacaille's creations. He called it "Pyxis Nautica" (The Nautical Box, or Mariner's Compass).

Reticulum

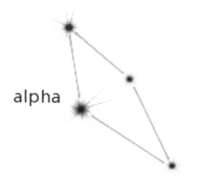

alpha

THE RETICULE

Reticulum was introduced by Nicolas Louis de Lacaille in the mid 1700s, meant to commemorate the reticule, an instrument used by Lacaille to measure star positions.

Sagitta

Sham

THE ARROW

Sagitta, "The Arrow", while small and insignificant, is a constellation known to the Greeks. Some references believe that Sagittarius, the Archer, shot the arrow (apparently without a known target); others talk about Cupid, and Heracles, and Apollo. The point is, there isn't any established myth associated with Sagitta.

Sagittarius

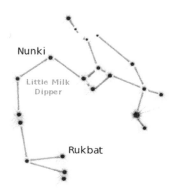

Nunki

Little Milk
Dipper

Rukbat

THE ARCHER

The zodiacal constellation Sagittarius represents the centaur Chiron. Most of the centaurs were regarded in myth as bestial--they were, after all, half horse. However, the ancient Greeks had a great deal of respect for the horse, and so were reluctant to make the centaurs entirely bad. In fact, Chiron was renowned for his gentleness. He was an excellent archer, musician, and physician, and tutored the likes of Achilles, Jason, and Heracles.

Chiron, however, was accidentally shot and wounded by Heracles. The arrow, which had been dipped in the poison of the Lernaean Hydra, inflicted great suffering on Chiron--so great, in fact, that even the talented physician could not cure himself. In agony, but as an immortal unable to find release in death, Chiron instead offered himself as a substitute for Prometheus. The gods had punished Prometheus for giving fire to man by chaining him to a rock. Each day an eagle would devour his liver, and each night it would grow back.

Scorpius

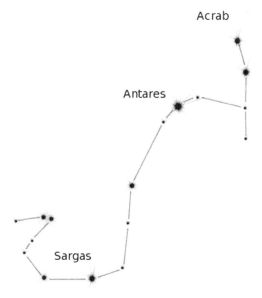

Acrab

Antares

Sargas

THE SCORPION

Scorpius is a zodiacal constellation. The scorpion is generally believed to be responsible for the death of the great hunter Orion. According to some myths, the scorpion stung Orion in response to his boast that he could defeat any beast; according to others, it was sent by Apollo, who was concerned for his sister Artemis's continued chastity.

In either case, Scorpius was placed in the opposite side of the sky from Orion so as to avoid any further conflict. It is to the southeast of Libra, and is marked by the bright red star Antares. (Antares is Greek for "Rival of Ares," the Greek war-god. The star is so named because of of its brightness and color, which are approximately the same as of the planet Mars.

Sculptor

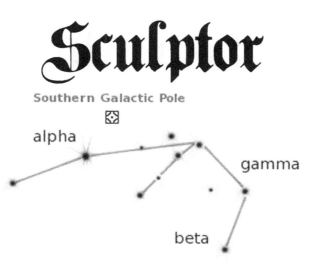

Southern Galactic Pole

alpha

gamma

beta

THE SCULPTOR

Sculptor is one of those obscure constellations invented by Nicolas Louis de Lacaille to help fill in part of the southern sky. The full name was "L'Atelier du Sculpteur", the Sculptor's Studio.

Scutum

Loannina

THE SHIELD

$\mathfrak{S}$cutum was invented by the Polish astronomer Johannes Hevelius, and was placed in his posthumous catalog of 1690, the Prodromus Astronomiae, along with Canes Venatici, Lacerta, Leo Minor, Lynx, Sextans, and Vulpecula.

These newer constellations became better known after being accepted by John Flamsteed in his catalog published in 1725.

The proper name is Scutum Sobiescianum, Sobieski's Shield, as the constellation pays honour to Jan Sobieski.

Jan Sobieski (1629-1696) was the eldest son of the castellan of Crakow, Jakob Sobieski. He was a brilliant military leader and by 1665 had become the field commander of the Polish army.

The main threat to Poland at this time (indeed to all of

central Europe) came from the Turks. While Sobieski attempted to repulse the Turks, the Polish king's envoys ceded all the Ukraine to Turkey. Meanwhile Sobieski won victory after victory. In November of 1673 the king died. Sobieski left the front lines and presented himself as a candidate for the throne back in Warsaw. (The kingship was an elected position.) In May of 1674 he became King John (or Jan) III.

Sobieski returned to his former job as army commander, and after nearly a ten year struggle, he was able to sign the Treaty of Warsaw with Leopold I. Following this treaty, Sobieski further safeguarded Europe from the Turks. Personally leading the Polish cavalry, on 12 September 1683, he broke the Turkish siege on Vienna, and liberated Hungary in the bargain.

Seven years later Hevelius commemorated these events with the inclusion of Scutum Sobiescianum in the heavens.

Serpens

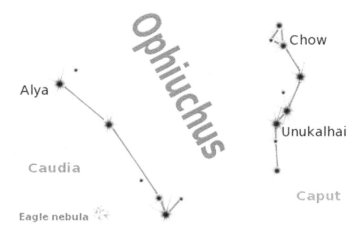

THE SERPENT

This is the second part of the Ophiuchus- Serpens group. The Serpent is being grasped in the hands of Ophiuchus the Serpent Holder. Thus the constellation wraps around Ophiuchus, and is divided into two parts: Serpens Caput (the head) and Serpens Cauda (the tail).

Sextans

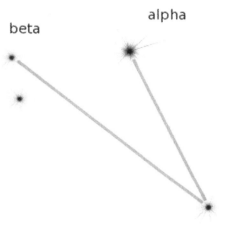

alpha

beta

THE SEXTANT

Sextans, "The Sextant" is one of a number of constellations devised by Johannes Hevelius, and published posthumously in 1690.

Taurus

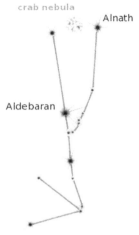

crab nebula

Alnath

Aldebaran

THE BULL

Taurus is a zodiacal constellation. According to myth, Taurus represents the bull-form taken on by Zeus when he became enamored of Europa, princess of Phoenicia:

Majesty and love go ill together, nor can they long share one abode. Abandoning the dignity of his sceptre, the father and ruler of the gods, whose hand wields the flaming three-forked bolt, whose nod shakes the universe, adopted the guise of a bull; and mingling with the other bullocks, joined in their lowing and ambled in the tender grass, a fair sight to see. His hide was white as untrodden snow, snow not yet melted by the rainy South wind. The muscles stood out on his neck, and deep folds of skin hung along his flanks. His horns were small, it is true, but so beautifully made that you would swear they were the work of an artist, more polished and shining than any jewel. There was no menace in the set of his head or in his eyes; he looked completely placid.(Metamorphoses II 847-858).

The princess Europa was impressed by the beauty and gentleness of the bull, and the two played together on the beach. Eventually, Europa climbed onto the bull's back, and he swam out to sea with her. He took her to Crete and revealed his true self.

The constellation Taurus consists of only the head and shoulders of the snowy white bull. The representation in the stars seems to show a raging bull, however, always about to plunge into Orion, which doesn't seem to reflect the gentle, seductive bull in Ovid's telling of the story.

Telescopium

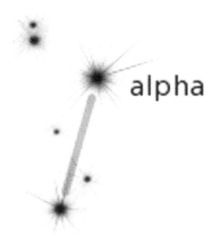

alpha

THE TELESCOPE

It is a shame that the most important instrument for astronomers should be associated with such a tiny portion of the sky, practically devoid of telescopic interest. Lacaille devised the constellation in the mid-eighteenth century.

Triangulum

Deltotum

Mothallah

THE TRIANGLE

Triangulum lies just to the north of Aries. In antiquity its distinctive shape of three stars was called Deltoton.

Triangulum Australe

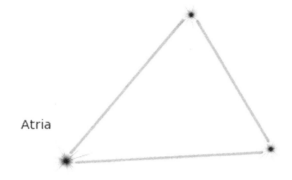

Atria

THE SOUTHERN TRIANGLE

Triangulum Australe, "The Southern Triangle", is one of the few constellations which has an obvious asterism. It was introduced by Johann Bayer in 1603.

Tucana

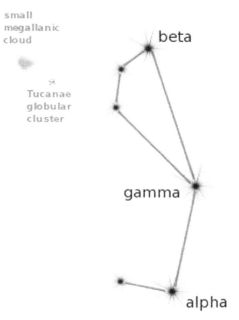

small
megallanic
cloud

47
Tucanae
globular
cluster

beta

gamma

alpha

THE TOUCAN

The toucan is a brightly coloured bird of Central and South America, known for its over-large beak. Talkative and friendly, it makes a nice pet. Just feed it fruit and insects, along with the occasional lizard, and it will love you for life.

In the skies the Toucan is one of three exotic birds which are grouped around the South Pole. The other two are Pavo (the Peacock) and Apus (Bird of Paradise).

All three were introduced by Johann Bayer, an amateur astronomer from Augsburg, Germany.

Bayer's book Uranometria, published in 1603, had an enormous effect on astronomy, for a number of reasons. First, it was the first book to treat the entire skies; all star atlases thus far had only looked at the northern hemisphere and patches of the southern. In order to cover the entire southern hemisphere Bayer had to fill in some of the blanks. So he adopted a number of constellations that others had invented, and put them in his book. In all, he introduced a dozen new constellations.

With the labeling of a constellation's stars with the Greek alphabet, hundreds more stars were instantly named. Unfortunately many southern hemisphere constellations haven't received Bayer letters, and instead go under a very awkward naming system. But by and large, Bayer's system of labelling stars has been very convenient indeed.

The Toucan is one of the circumpolar southern constellations. If you live north of Mexico City or Bombay you won't find it. It has few Bayer stars, mostly at the four to five-magnitude range.

Ursa Major

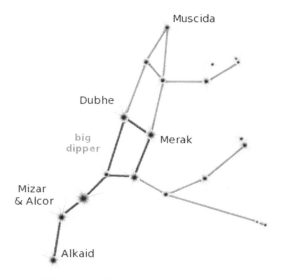

THE GREAT BEAR

The wood-nymph Callisto was a maiden in the wild region Arcadia. She was a huntress, "not one who spent her time in spinning soft fibers of wool, or in arranging her hair in different styles. She was one of Artemis' warriors, wearing her tunic pinned together with a brooch, her tresses carelessly caught back by a white ribbon, and carrying in her hand a light javelin or her bow" (Metamorphoses II 412-415).

Zeus caught sight of her and immediately desired her. He took on the shape of the goddess Artemis and spoke to Callisto, who was delighted to see the form of her mistress. She began to tell him of her hunting exploits, and he responded by raping her. "She resisted him as far as a woman could--had Hera seen her she would have been less cruel--but how could a girl overcome a man, and who could defeat Zeus? He had his way, and returned to the upper air" (Metamorphoses II 434-437).

The cruelty of Hera mentioned by Ovid resulted from the goddess's easily-aroused jealousy. Unfortunate Callisto bore a son to Zeus, Arcas, infuriating Hera. Out of jealousy, the wife of Zeus transformed the girl into a bear. She lived for a time in the wild, until Arcas came across her one day while hunting. Unknowingly, he was about to kill his mother in her bear form, but Zeus took mercy on Callisto, stayed Arcas's hand, and transformed him into a lesser bear. The king of gods then placed both mother and son into the heavens as neighboring constellations.

The constellation Ursa Major, representing Callisto, is one of our most familiar. It includes the Big Dipper, perhaps the most-recognized feature of a constellation in the heavens

Ursa Minor

Polaris

Kochab

Pherkad

THE LESSER BEAR

Arcas was the son of Callisto, who was transformed by Hera into a bear. When Arcas was fifteen, he was out hunting in the forest when he came across a bear. The bear behaved quite strangely, looking him in the eyes. He of course could not recognize his mother in her strange shape, and was preparing to shoot her when Zeus prevented him. Arcas was transformed into a bear like his mother, and the two were taken up into the sky. Hera was annoyed that the pair should be given such honor, and took her revenge by convincing Poseidon to forbid them from bathing in the sea. It is for this reason that Ursa Major and Ursa Minor are both circumpolar constellations, never dipping beneath the horizon when viewed from northern latitudes.

Ursa Minor is better known as the Little Dipper.

Vela

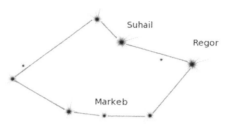

Suhail
Regor
Markeb

THE SAIL

As mentioned in regard to "Carina", Jason and his Argonauts sailed off in the Argo Navis to capture the Golden Fleece. The constellation that commemorated that adventure is now broken up into three smaller constellations: Carina (the Keel), Puppis (the Stern) and Vela (the Sail).

The stars that make up the sail are widely dispersed. Some cartographers of the night sky add a few more stars to make the sail more billowy. Since Vela is part of the original Argo Navis, it has only a few of the Bayer stars of that larger constellation.

Sometimes observers associate the lower two stars, kappa Velorum and delta Velorum, with iota Carinae and epsilon Carinae, and believe they are looking at the Southern Cross. The real Southern Cross is in the nearby constellation of Crux; this cross shared by Vela and Carina goes by the name of the False Cross.

Although Vela does not make much of a sight in the southern skies, it does have a number of notable objects, including the brightest Wolf-Rayet star, an optical pulsar, and a pulsating variable which is the prototype of an entire class of cepheids.

Virgo

The Virgin

Virgo is a zodiacal constellation. According to the ancient poets, the virgin is also sometimes known as Astraea. She lived on the earth during the Golden Age of man, which is described by Hesiod:

First a golden race of mortal men were
made by the immortals who have Olympian homes.
  They lived in Kronos' [Saturn's] time, when he ruled the
sky,
  they lived like gods, with carefree heart,
free and apart from trouble and pain; grim old age
did not afflict them, but with arms and legs always
strong they played in delight, apart from all evils;
They died as if subdued by sleep; and all good things
were theirs; the fertile earth produced fruit
by itself, abundantly and unforced; willingly and

effortlessly they ruled their lands with many goods.
But since the earth hid this race below,
they are daimones by the plans of great Zeus [Zeus],
benevolent earthly guardians of mortal men,
who watch over judgments and cruel deeds,
clothed in air and roaming over all the earth
(Works and Days 109-125).

The "daimones" of which Hesiod speaks are invisible spirits which watch over men. Presumably, although it is unclear, Astraea is the daimone whose province is justice. The emblem of her office was therefore the scales (Libra), which are seen next to Virgo in the sky.

Virgo is the second largest constellation and is highest in the northern hemisphere during May and June. The brightest star in Virgo is Spica.

Mythology, of course, influenced the naming of many objects in the night sky, not just the constellations. The planets all bear names from Roman mythology which reflect their characteristics: Mercury, named for the speedy messenger god, revolves fastest around the sun; Venus, named for the goddess of love and beauty, shines most brightly; Mars, named for the god of war, appears blood-red; Zeus, named for the single most important god, is the largest planet in our solar system. Even the names of the Galilean moons of Zeus (the four largest, which may be seen with even a small telescope) are drawn from mythology. Io, Europa, Ganymede, and Callisto were all desired--and taken by force--by Zeus. It is ironic that the mythological characters mythological women the king of the gods so ardently pursued now revolve around him.

Volans

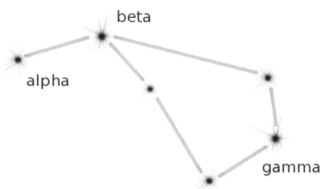

beta

alpha

gamma

THE FLYING FISH

Volans is one of those constellations introduced by Johann Bayer in his 1603 star atlas. He called it Piscis Volans; only the adjective has survived. The asterism shows a sideways view of the "flying fish" (sort of).

𝔙ulpecula

Anser

THE FOX

𝔙ulpecula, The Fox, is one of Johannes Hevelius' constellations, introduced in his posthumously published star catalog of 1690. (See "Lacerta" for comments on Hevelius.) The asterism resembles more a flying gull seen face on.

The constellation was originally called Vulpecula cum Anser, The Fox and Goose.

OTHER BOOKS BY
ERROL CODER

The Ancestral Families
of the Greek Gods and their kin, Summer 2012

When Titans Roamed, Summer 2012

Made in the USA
Monee, IL
16 December 2021

85830893R00069